Elizabeth's Tuition Centre

Bond

10 Minute Tests

10-11 years

Alison Primrose

Non-verbal Reasoning

Nelson Thornes
a Wolters Kluwer business

TEST 1: **Sequences and Codes**

Which pattern continues or completes the given series?

Example

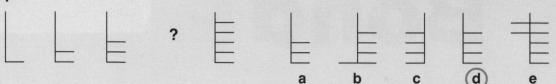

1

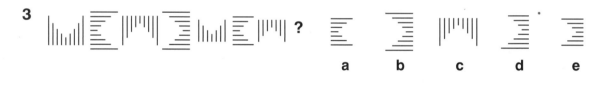

2

3

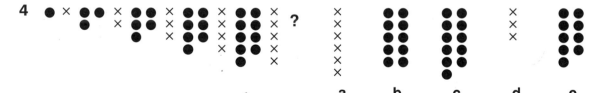

4

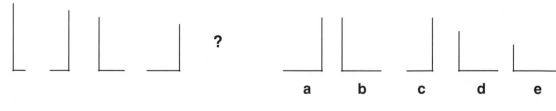

5

6

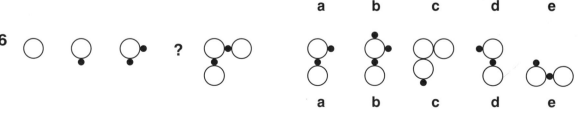

Using the given patterns and codes, select the code that matches the last pattern.

Example

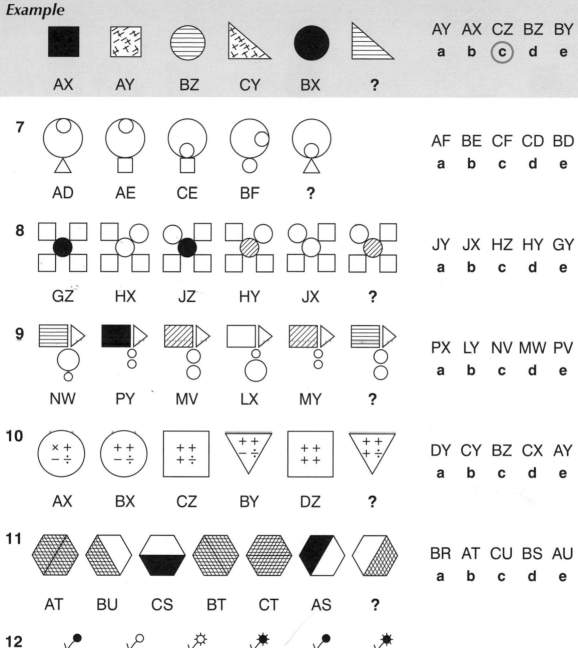

Example

AX   AY   BZ   CY   BX   ?

AY AX CZ BZ BY
a   b   ⓒ   d   e

7

AD   AE   CE   BF   ?

AF BE CF CD BD
a   b   c   d   e

8

GZ   HX   JZ   HY   JX   ?

JY JX HZ HY GY
a   b   c   d   e

9

NW   PY   MV   LX   MY   ?

PX LY NV MW PV
a   b   c   d   e

10

AX   BX   CZ   BY   DZ   ?

DY CY BZ CX AY
a   b   c   d   e

11

AT   BU   CS   BT   CT   AS   ?

BR AT CU BS AU
a   b   c   d   e

12

AX   BZ   DY   CZ   AY   ?

AZ BZ CX DX CY
a   b   c   d   e

3

Total

Using the given patterns and codes, select the code that matches the last pattern.

Example

AX   AY   BZ   CY   BX   ?

AY AX CZ BZ BY
a   b   ⓒ   d   e

1

BX   CY   AZ   CX   DZ   ?

AX AY CZ DY BZ
a   b   c   d   e

2

ER   DR   ES   FR   FT   ?

ET FS DS DT ES
a   b   c   d   e

3

AH   BJ   AG   BK   CG   ?

CH BG CJ AK BH
a   b   c   d   e

4

LX   MY   LZ   NY   MZ   ?

LY NZ NX MX NY
a   b   c   d   e   .

5

AX   BY   CZ   BZ   DY   ?

CX CY BZ DZ AY
a   b   c   d   e

6

AY   BX   CZ   AX   BZ   DY   ?

AZ BY DX DZ CY
a   b   c   d   e

Which shape or pattern completes the second pair in the same way as the first pair?

Example

a   b   c   (d)   e

7

a   b   c   d   e

8

a   b   c   d   e

9

a   b   c   d   e

10

a   b   c   d   e

11

a   b   c   d   e

12

a   b   c   d   e

Total

Which of the shapes belongs with the group on the left?

Example

a   b   c   ⓓ   e

1

a   b   c   d   e

2

a   b   c   d   e

3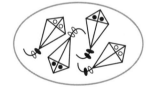

a   b   c   d   e

4

a   b   c   d   e

5

a   b   c   d   e

6

a   b   c   d   e

Which pattern completes the given grid?

Example

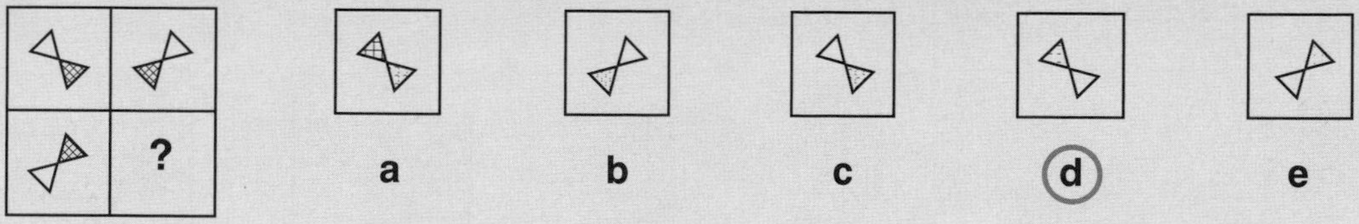

d

7

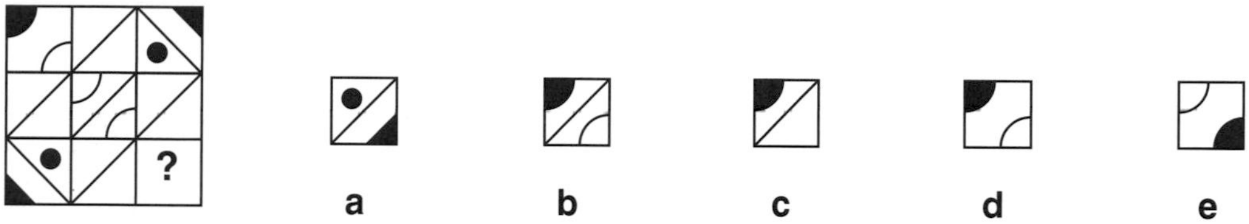

a   b   c   d   e

8

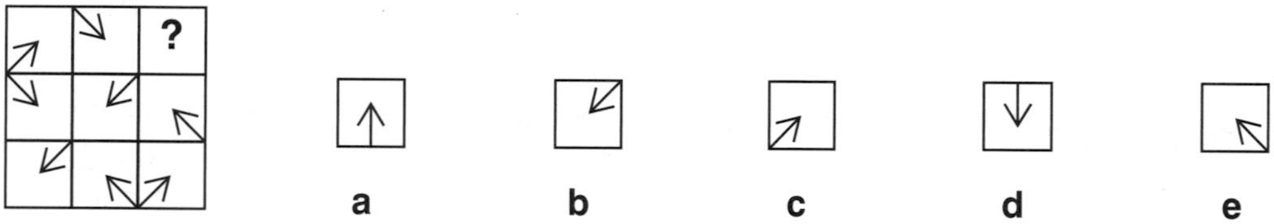

a   b   c   d   e

9

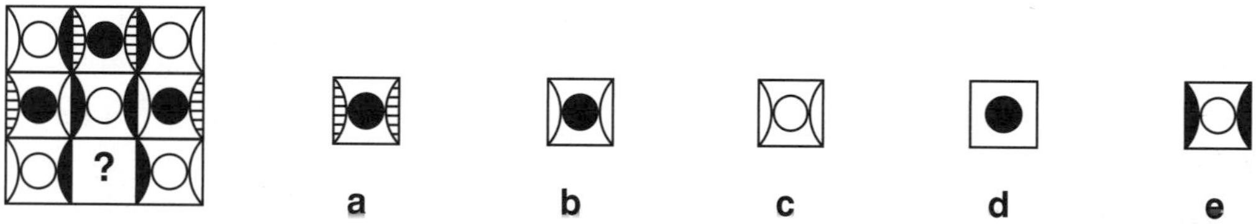

a   b   c   d   e

10

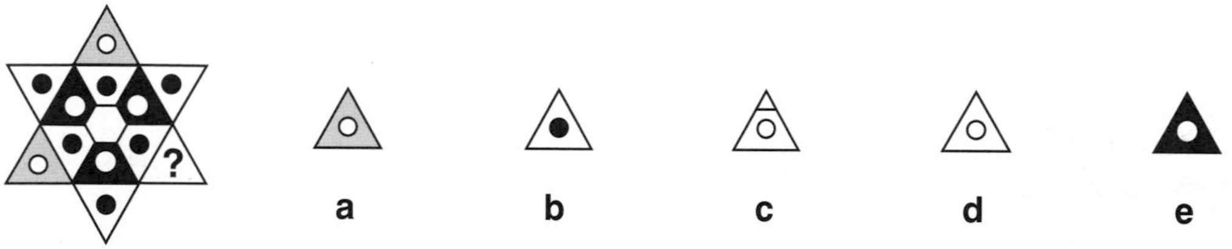

a   b   c   d   e

11

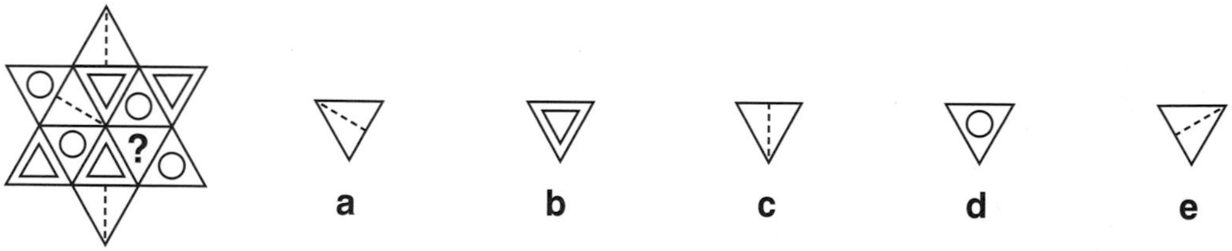

a   b   c   d   e

12

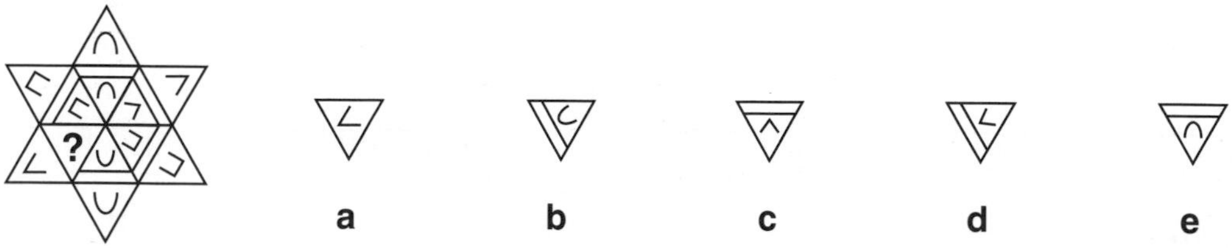

a   b   c   d   e

Total

Which pattern continues or completes the given series?

Example

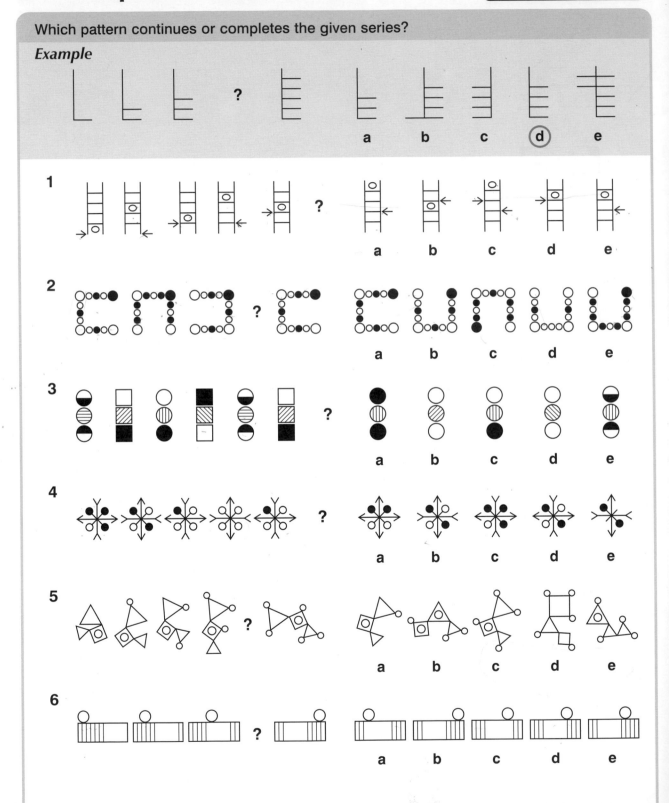

Using the given patterns and codes, select the code that matches the last pattern.

Example

AX   AY   BZ   CY   BX   ?

AY AX CZ BZ BY
a   b   (c)   d   e

7

XP   YR   ZS   XQ   YP   ?

ZR YS XS YQ ZQ
a   b   c   d   e

8

AN   BM   BL   AM   CO   ?

CN BN CL AO AL
a   b   c   d   e

9

BX   CX   AY   DX   BY   ?

DY CX CY AX DY
a   b   c   d   e

10

FM   EM   GL   EN   FL   ?

EL FN GN GM FM
a   b   c   d   e

11

AX   BY   AZ   CX   BZ   ?

AY BX CZ BY CY
a   b   c   d   e

12

DX   DW   EX   CZ   CY   ?

CW EW VX EY DZ
a   b   c   d   e

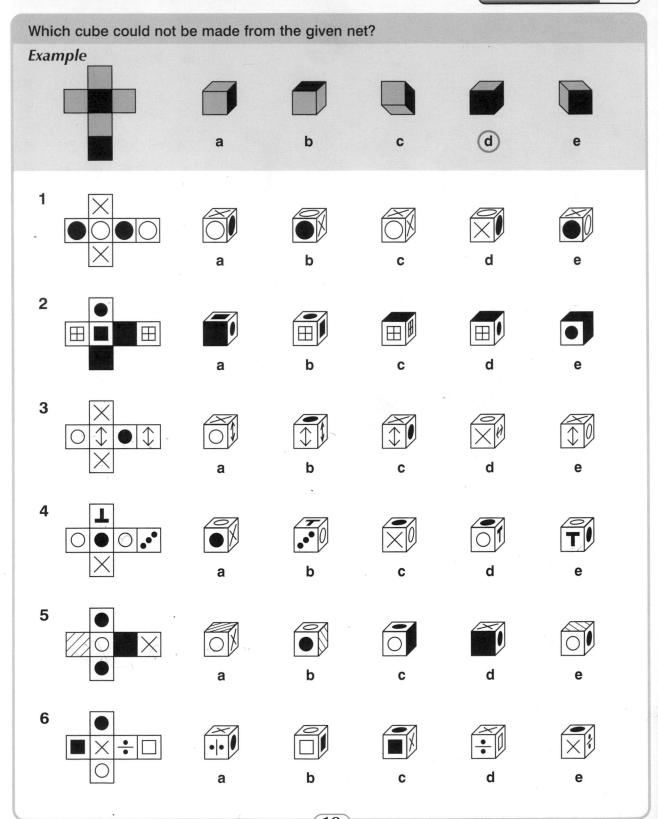

Which of the shapes belongs with the group on the left?

Example

a   b   c   (d)   e

7

a   b   c   d   e

8

a   b   c   d   e

9

a   b   c   d   e

10

a   b   c   d   e

11

a   b   c   d   e

12

a   b   c   d   e

Total

TEST 6: Codes and Analogies

Test time: 0 | | | | | 5 | | | | | 10 minutes

Using the given patterns and codes, select the code that matches the last pattern.

Example

AY AX CZ BZ BY
a b (c) d e

AX   AY   BZ   CY   BX   ?

1

CY BX CX AY DZ
a b c d e

AZ   BY   CZ   DX   AX   ?

2

CZ BY AZ AY BX
a b c d e

BX   AX   CY   BZ   CX   ?

3

DN DL EM EL FL
a b c d e

DM   EN   FN   EL   FM   ?

4

TE SH TH SE TF
a b c d e

SE   SF   TG   TH   SG   ?

5

QN PW PS PN QS
a b c d e

PS   QW   PE   QN   QE   ?

6

CH BF DF DH AF
a b c d e

AG   CF   BE   AH   DG   ?

12

Which shape or pattern completes the second pair in the same way as the first pair?

Example

[is to ⌐ as [is to] a b c (d) e

7 is to as is to a b c d e

8 is to as is to a b c d e

9 is to as is to a b c d e

10 is to as is to a b c d e

11 is to as is to a b c d e

12 is to as is to a b c d e

Total

TEST 7: Analogies and Cubes

Which shape or pattern completes the second pair in the same way as the first pair?

Example

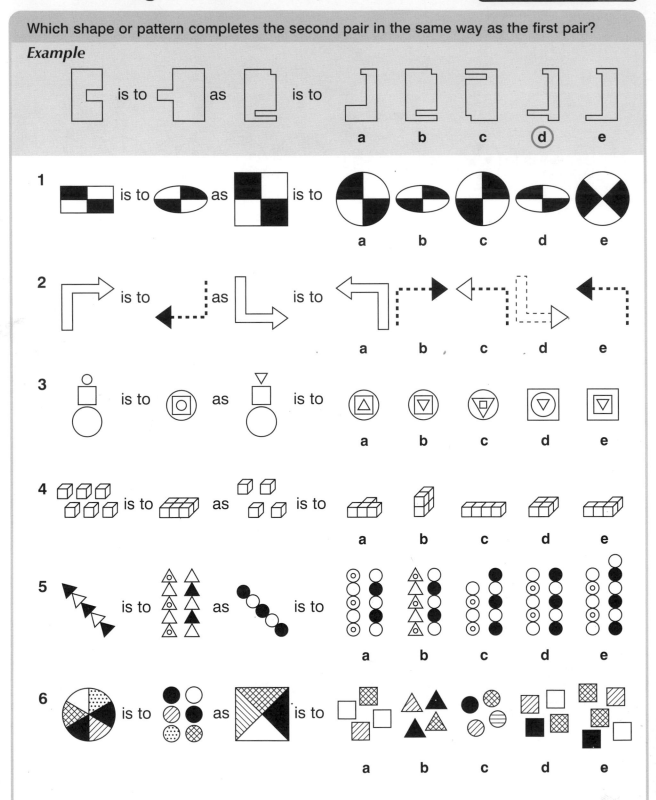

Which cube could not be made from the given net?

Example

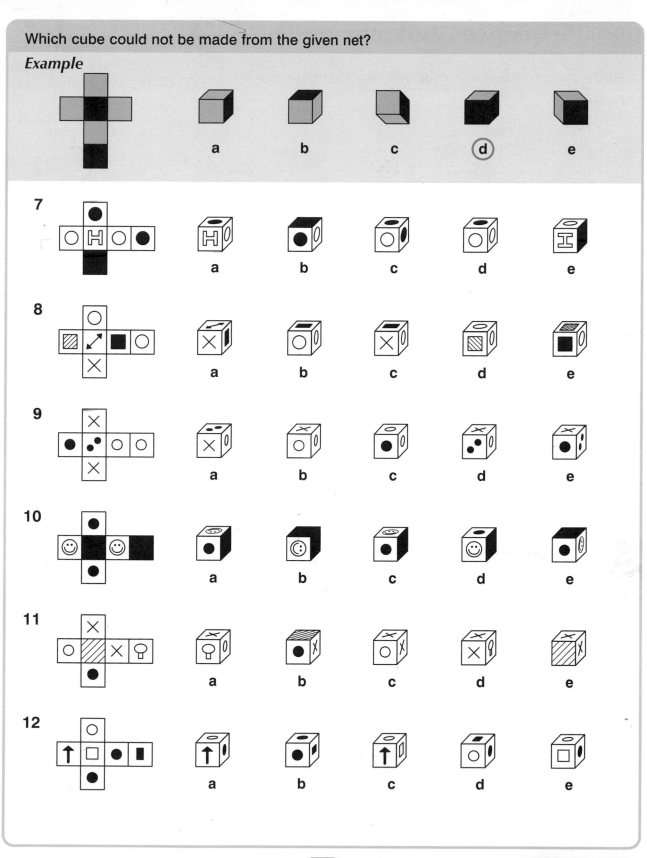

7

8

9

10

11

12

a   b   c   d   e

15

Total

Which pattern continues or completes the given series?

Example

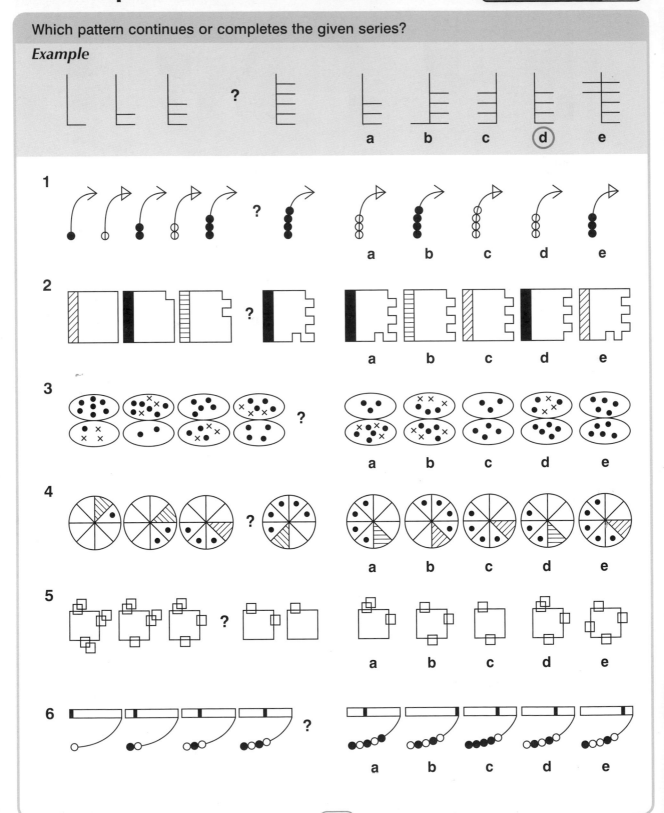

Which of the shapes belongs with the group on the left?

Example

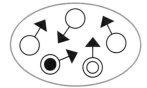

a   b   c   (d)   e

7   

a   b   c   d   e

8   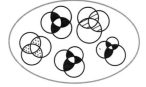

a   b   c   d   e

9   

a   b   c   d   e

10   

a   b   c   d   e

11   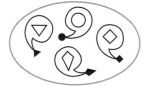

a   b   c   d   e

12   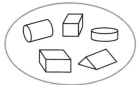

a   b   c   d   e

Time for a break! Go to Puzzle Page 43

Total

TEST 9: **Analogies and Similarities**

Which shape or pattern completes the second pair in the same way as the first pair?

Example

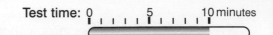

     a   b   c   (d)   e

1

a   b   c   d   e

2

a   b   c   d   e

3

a   b   c   d   e

4

a   b   c   d   e

5

a   b   c   d   e

6

a   b   c   d   e

Which of the shapes belongs with the group on the left?

Example

a   b   c   d   e

7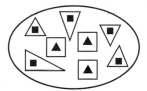

a   b   c   d   e

8

a   b   c   d   e

9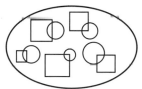

a   b   c   d   e

10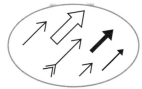

a   b   c   d   e

11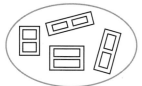

a   b   c   d   e

12

a   b   c   d   e

Total

Test time: 0 | | | | | | 5 | | | | 10 minutes

Using the given patterns and codes, select the code that matches the last pattern.

Example

AX   AY   BZ   CY   BX   ?

AY   AX   CZ   BZ   BY
a   b   (c)   d   e

1

XL   XM   YN   ZN   YM   ?

ZL   XN   XL   ZM   YL
a   b   c   d   e

2

LD   MG   NF   OD   ME   ?

OG   LE   NE   MF   ND
a   b   c   d   e

3

AT   BV   BU   CU   CT   ?

AT   AV   CV   BT   CU
a   b   c   d   e

4

FA   DB   GA   DC   EB   ?

EA   DA   GC   GB   FB
a   b   c   d   e

5

LX   MY   NY   NZ   MX   ?

LY   MX   NX   LX   MZ
a   b   c   d   e

6

BF   DG   CF   AG   DH   ?

AF   DF   CH   AH   BH
a   b   c   d   e

Which cube could not be made from the given net?

a　　b　　c　　(d)　　e

7

a　　b　　c　　d　　e

8

a　　b　　c　　d　　e

9

a　　b　　c　　d　　e

10

a　　b　　c　　d　　e

11

a　　b　　c　　d　　e

12

a　　b　　c　　d　　e

Total

Which of the shapes belongs with the group on the left?

1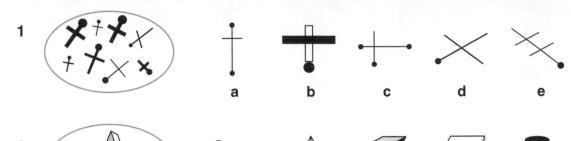

2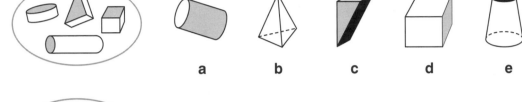

3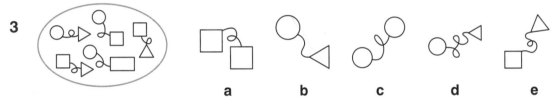

Which pattern continues or completes the given series?

4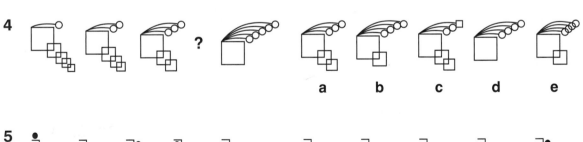

5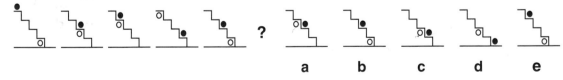

6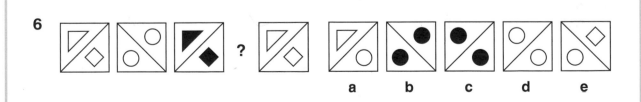

Which shape or pattern completes the second pair in the same way as the first pair?

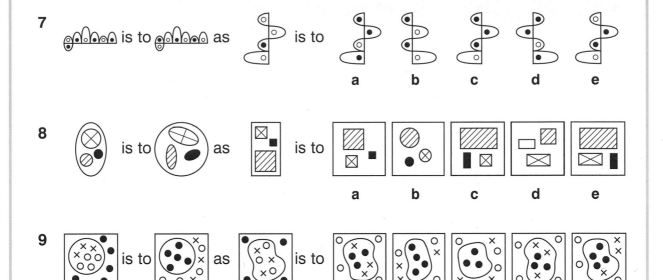

7 ⌒⌒⌒⌒⌒ is to ⌒⌒⌒⌒⌒ as [spiral] is to

a   b   c   d   e

8 is to as is to

a   b   c   d   e

9 is to as is to

a   b   c   d   e

Using the given patterns and codes, select the code that matches the last pattern.

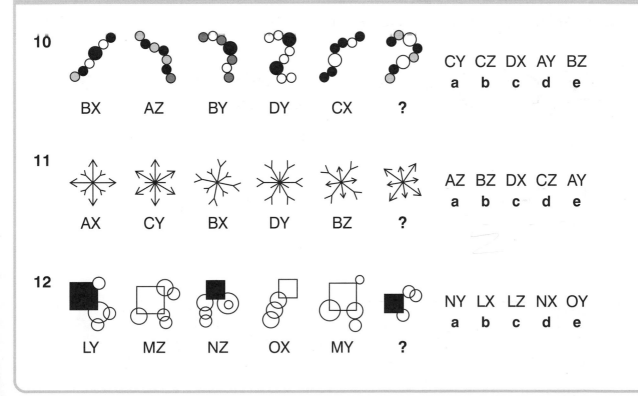

10

BX   AZ   BY   DY   CX   ?

CY CZ DX AY BZ
a   b   c   d   e

11

AX   CY   BX   DY   BZ   ?

AZ BZ DX CZ AY
a   b   c   d   e

12

LY   MZ   NZ   OX   MY   ?

NY LX LZ NX OY
a   b   c   d   e

Total

Which pattern continues or completes the given series?

1  **?**

                                        a   b   c   d   e

2 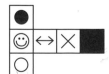 **?**

                                        a   b   c   d   e

3 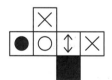 **?**

                                        a   b   c   d   e

Which cube could not be made from the given net?

4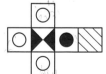

                                       a   b   c   d   e

5

                                       a   b   c   d   e

6

                                       a   b   c   d   e

Example

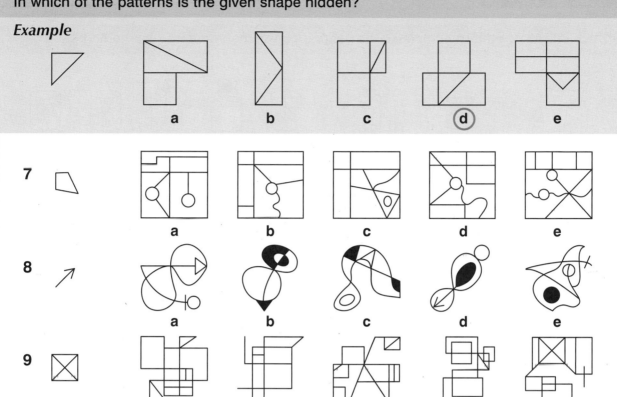

Using the given patterns and codes, select the code that matches the last pattern.

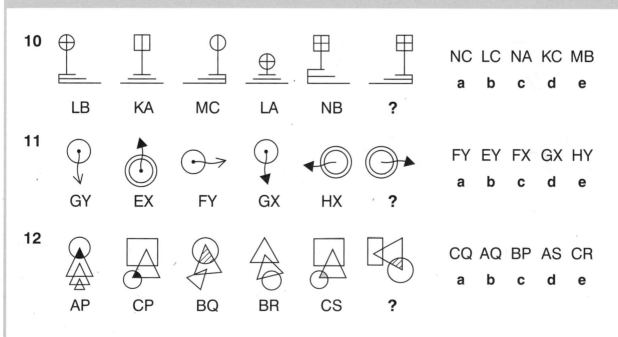

Test time: 0 |||||| 5 ||||| 10 minutes

Which shape or pattern completes the second pair in the same way as the first pair?

1   [flower in vase] is to [flower in vase] as [sun in glass] is to

a   b   c   d   e

2   [pattern] is to [pattern] as [pattern] is to

a   b   c   d   e

3   [symbols] is to [symbols] as [symbols] is to

a   b   c   d   e

Which of the shapes belongs with the group on the left?

4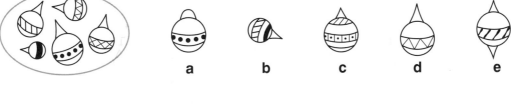

a   b   c   d   e

5   [group of shapes]

a   b   c   d   e

6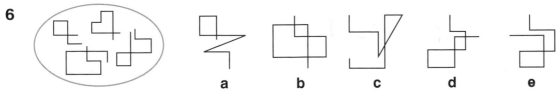

a   b   c   d   e

26

Which is the mirror image of the shape on the left?

Example

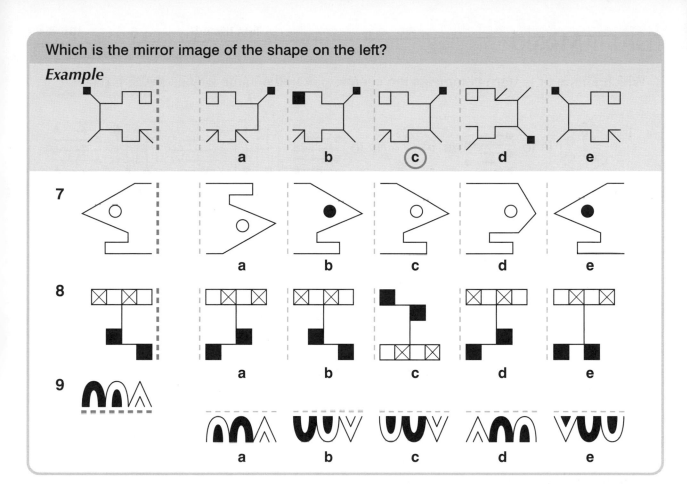

a   b   c   d   e

7

a   b   c   d   e

8

a   b   c   d   e

9

a   b   c   d   e

Which pattern continues or completes the given series?

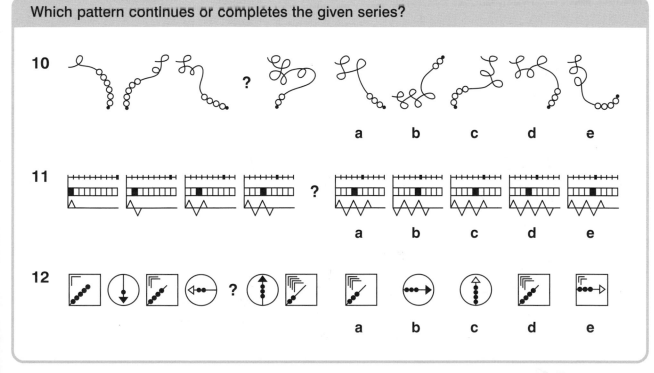

10

? a b c d e

11

? a b c d e

12

? a b c d e

Total

Which shape or pattern completes the second pair in the same way as the first pair?

1

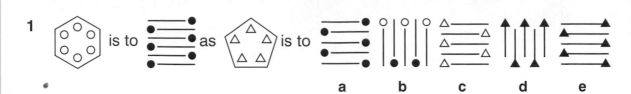

a   b   c   d   e

2

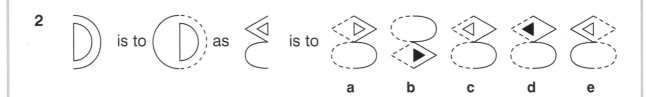

a   b   c   d   e

3

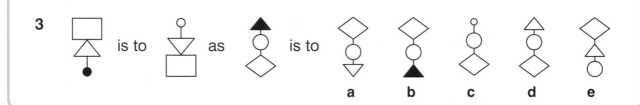

a   b   c   d   e

Which of the shapes belongs with the group on the left?

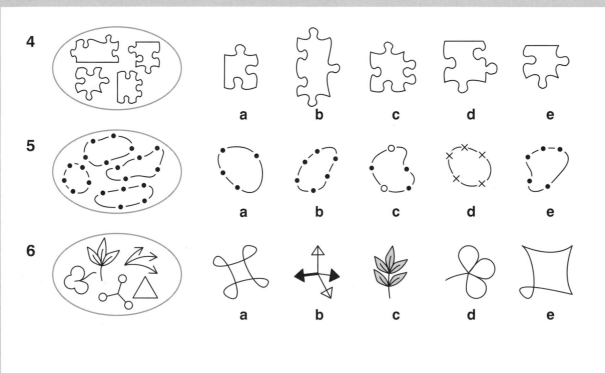

4

a   b   c   d   e

5

a   b   c   d   e

6

a   b   c   d   e

Using the given patterns and codes, select the code that matches the last pattern.

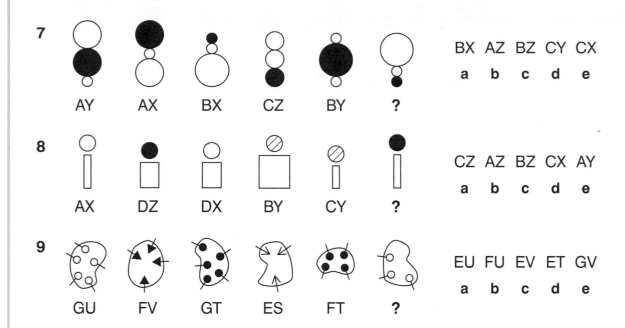

7   AY   AX   BX   CZ   BY   ?

BX AZ BZ CY CX
 a   b   c   d   e

8   AX   DZ   DX   BY   CY   ?

CZ AZ BZ CX AY
 a   b   c   d   e

9   GU   FV   GT   ES   FT   ?

EU FU EV ET GV
 a   b   c   d   e

Which cube could not be made from the given net?

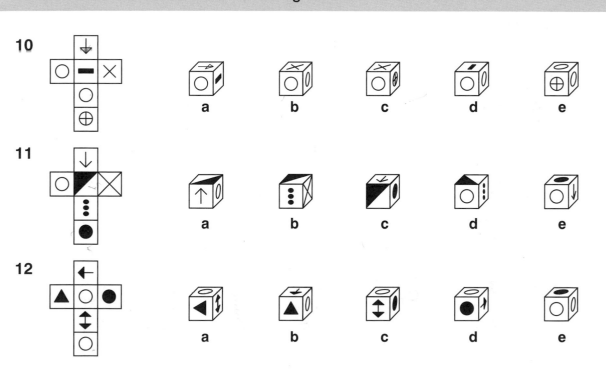

10   a   b   c   d   e

11   a   b   c   d   e

12   a   b   c   d   e

Total

Which pattern continues or completes the given series?

1

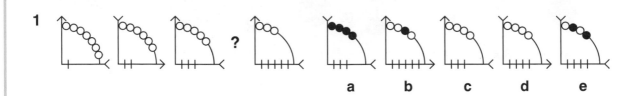

                    a   b   c   d   e

2

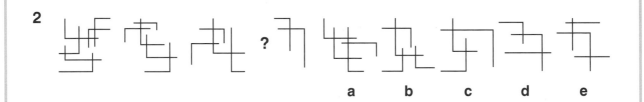

                    a   b   c   d   e

3

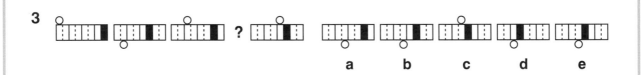

                    a   b   c   d   e

Using the given patterns and codes, select the code that matches the last pattern.

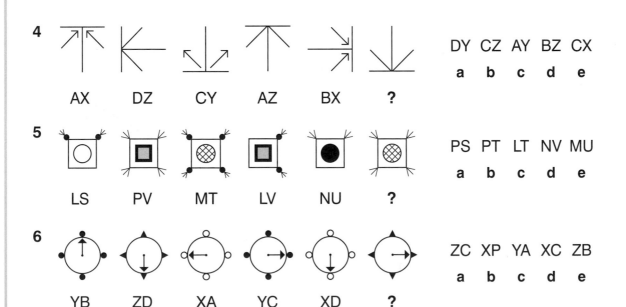

4

DY CZ AY BZ CX
a   b   c   d   e

AX   DZ   CY   AZ   BX   ?

5

PS PT LT NV MU
a   b   c   d   e

LS   PV   MT   LV   NU   ?

6

ZC XP YA XC ZB
a   b   c   d   e

YB   ZD   XA   YC   XD   ?

In which of the patterns is the given shape hidden?

7

   a   **b**   **c**   **d**   **e**

8

   a   **b**   **c**   **d**   **e**

9

   a   **b**   **c**   **d**   **e**

Which of the shapes belongs with the group on the left?

10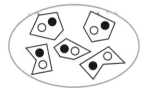

   a   **b**   **c**   **d**   **e**

11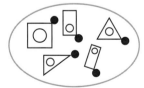

   a   **b**   **c**   **d**   **e**

12

   a   **b**   **c**   **d**   **e**

Total

Which cube could not be made from the given net?

1 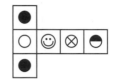 a b c d e

2 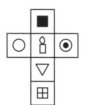 a b c d e

3 a b c d e

Which shape or pattern completes the second pair in the same way as the first pair?

4 is to as is to

a b c d e

5 is to as is to

a b c d e

6   is to as is to

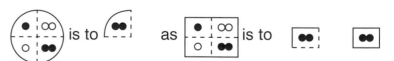

a b c d e

Which of the shapes belongs with the group on the left?

7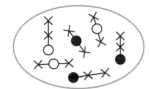

    a   b   c   d   e

8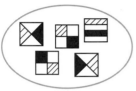

    a   b   c   d   e

9

    a   b   c   d   e

Which is the mirror image of the shape on the left?

10

    a   b   c   d   e

11

    a   b   c   d   e

12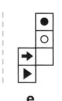

    a   b   c   d   e

Using the given patterns and codes, select the code that matches the last pattern.

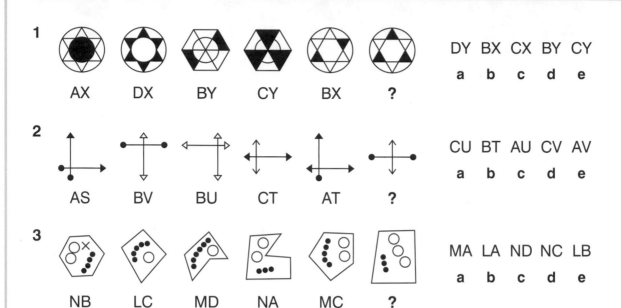

1

AX   DX   BY   CY   BX   ?

DY BX CX BY CY
a   b   c   d   e

2

AS   BV   BU   CT   AT   ?

CU BT AU CV AV
a   b   c   d   e

3

NB   LC   MD   NA   MC   ?

MA LA ND NC LB
a   b   c   d   e

Which shape or pattern completes the second pair in the same way as the first pair?

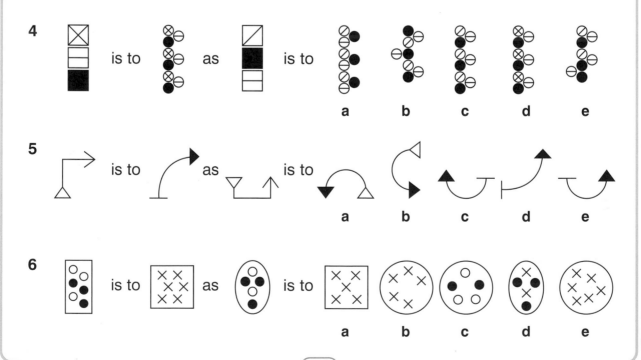

4   is to   as   is to

a   b   c   d   e

5   is to   as   is to

a   b   c   d   e

6   is to   as   is to

a   b   c   d   e

Which pattern continues or completes the given series?

7 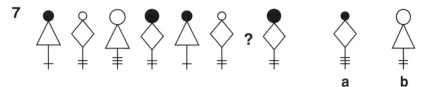 **?**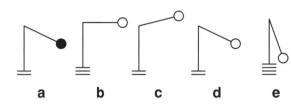

a   b   c   d   e

8 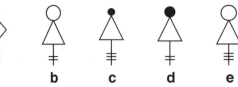 **?**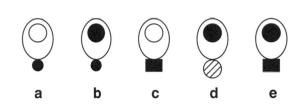

a   b   c   d   e

9

a   b   c   d   e

Which of the shapes belongs with the group on the left?

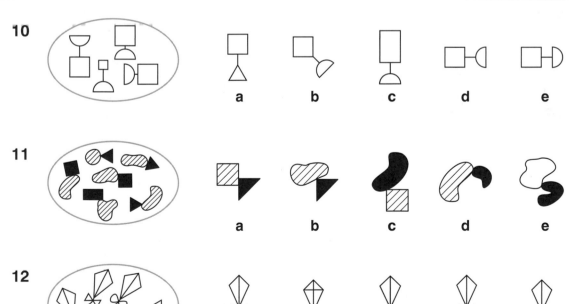

10

a   b   c   d   e

11

a   b   c   d   e

12

a   b   c   d   e

Total

Test 18: **Mixed**

Using the given patterns and codes, select the code that matches the last pattern.

1

AY   BZ   CZ   AX   DY   ?

CY CX BY AZ DX
a b c d e

2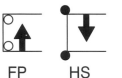

FP   HS   GR   HQ   GP   ?

GQ HP FS HR FR
a b c d e

3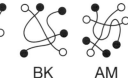

AJ   BK   AM   BL   CK   ?

BM AK CJ BJ CL
a b c d e

Which shape or pattern completes the second pair in the same way as the first pair?

4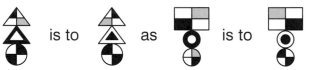

a   b   c   d   e

5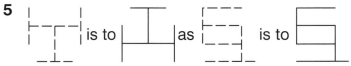

a   b   c   d   e

6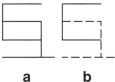

a   b   c   d   e

Which pattern continues or completes the given series?

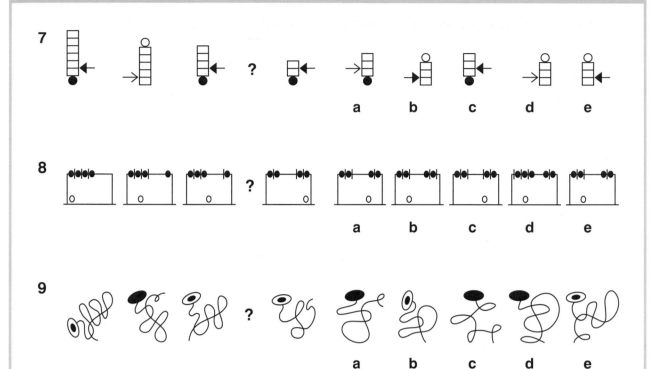

7

8

9

a   b   c   d   e

Which cube could not be made from the given net?

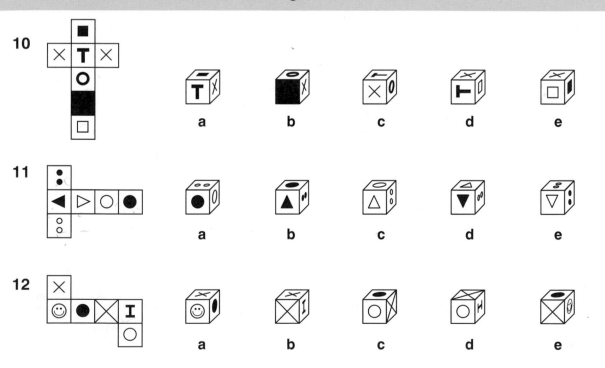

10

a   b   c   d   e

11

a   b   c   d   e

12

a   b   c   d   e

Total

Which of the shapes belongs with the group on the left?

1

     a   b   c   d   e

2

     a   b   c   d   e

3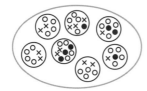

     a   b   c   d   e

In which of the patterns is the given shape hidden?

4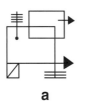

     a   b   c   d   e

5

     a   b   c   d   e

6

     a   b   c   d   e

Using the given patterns and codes, select the code that matches the last pattern.

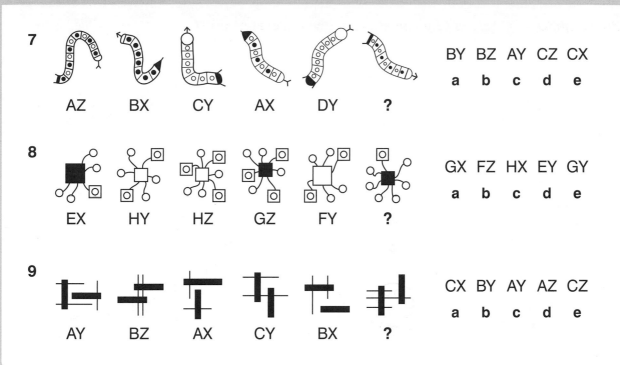

7

AZ   BX   CY   AX   DY   ?

BY BZ AY CZ CX
a   b   c   d   e

8

EX   HY   HZ   GZ   FY   ?

GX FZ HX EY GY
a   b   c   d   e

9

AY   BZ   AX   CY   BX   ?

CX BY AY AZ CZ
a   b   c   d   e

Which is the mirror image of the shape on the left?

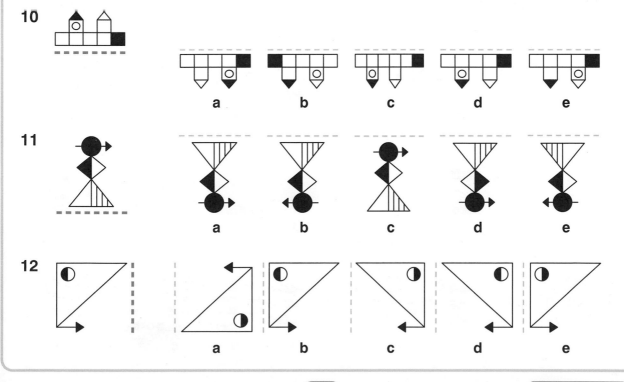

10

a   b   c   d   e

11

a   b   c   d   e

12

a   b   c   d   e

Total

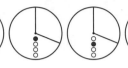

Which pattern continues or completes the given series or grid?

1 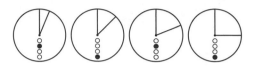 ?

       a   b   c   d   e

2

       a   b   c   d   e

3  ?

       a   b   c   d   e

Which shape or pattern completes the second pair in the same way as the first pair?

4 is to  as is to

       a   b   c   d   e

5 is to as is to

       a   b   c   d   e

6 is to as is to

       a   b   c   d   e

Which cube could not be made from the given net?

7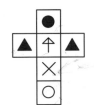

           a   **b**   **c**   **d**   **e**

8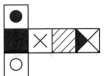

           a   **b**   **c**   **d**   **e**

9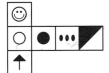

           a   **b**   **c**   **d**   **e**

Which of the shapes belongs with the group on the left?

10

           a   **b**   **c**   **d**   **e**

11

           a   **b**   **c**   **d**   **e**

12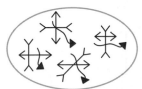

           a   **b**   **c**   **d**   **e**

Total

Puzzle ①

Circle the two sets of parallel lines that are not equal in length.

A

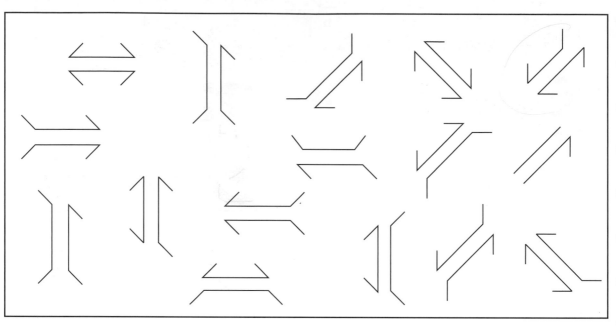

In which pattern is the bold square bigger than the white square in the middle.

B

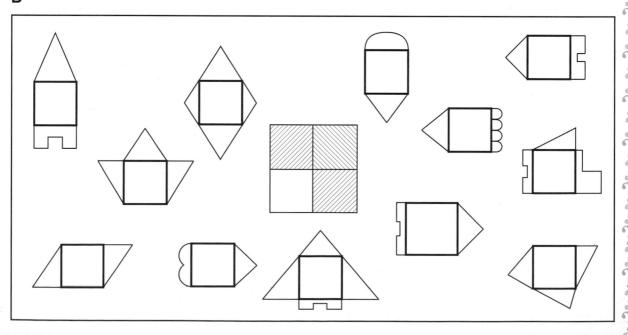

Puzzle ❷

In each box circle the pattern that is different from the rest.

A

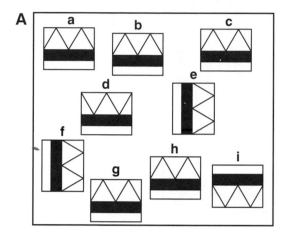

B

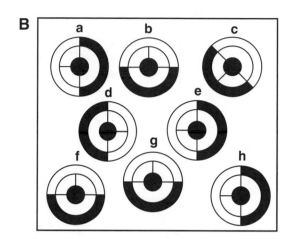

C

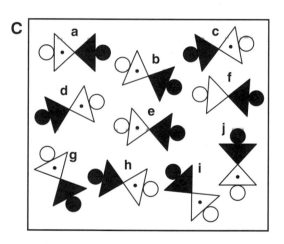

D

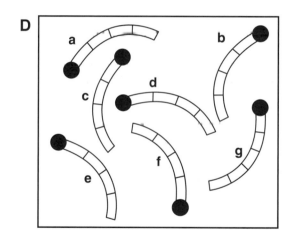

E

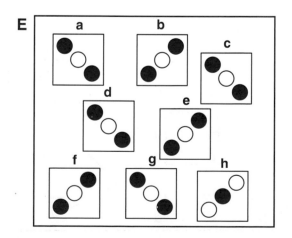

F

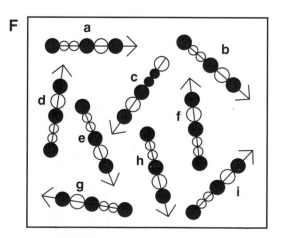

Puzzle ③

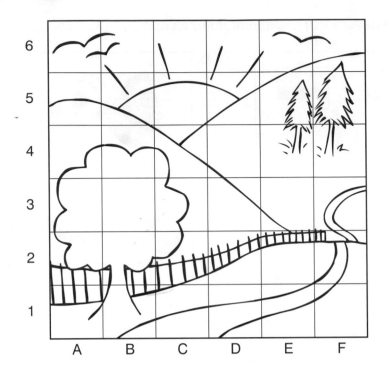

Which grid square is drawn below?

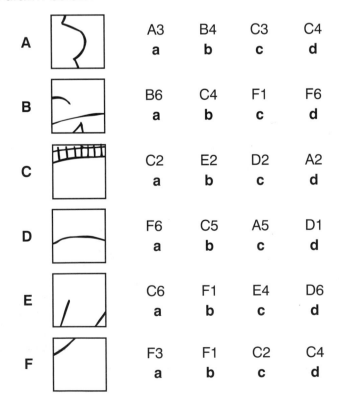

| | | A3 a | B4 b | C3 c | C4 d |
| **A** | | | | | |

| | | B6 a | C4 b | F1 c | F6 d |
| **B** | | | | | |

| | | C2 a | E2 b | D2 c | A2 d |
| **C** | | | | | |

| | | F6 a | C5 b | A5 c | D1 d |
| **D** | | | | | |

| | | C6 a | F1 b | E4 c | D6 d |
| **E** | | | | | |

| | | F3 a | F1 b | C2 c | C4 d |
| **F** | | | | | |

Puzzle ④

Identify and link the shapes that form a pair, in the same way as the pair already joined.

A

Join each shape on the left with its mirror image on the right.

B

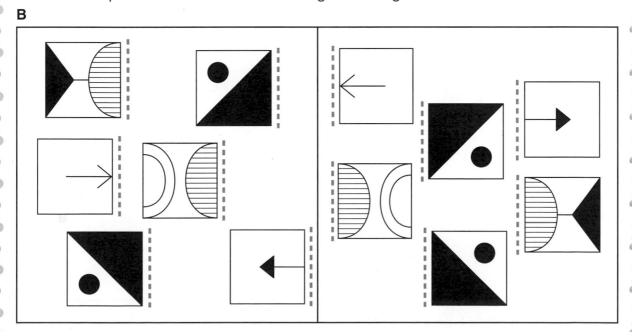

Puzzle ⑤

Complete these patterns by drawing their reflection in the dotted mirror line.
The first one has been started for you:

A

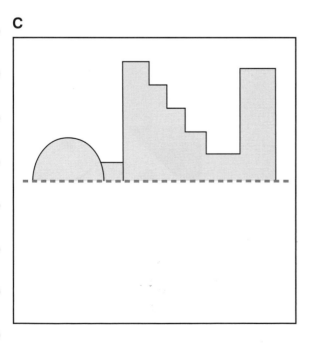

B

C

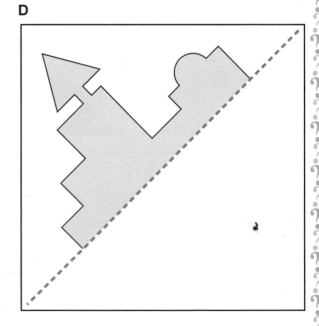

D

Progress Grid

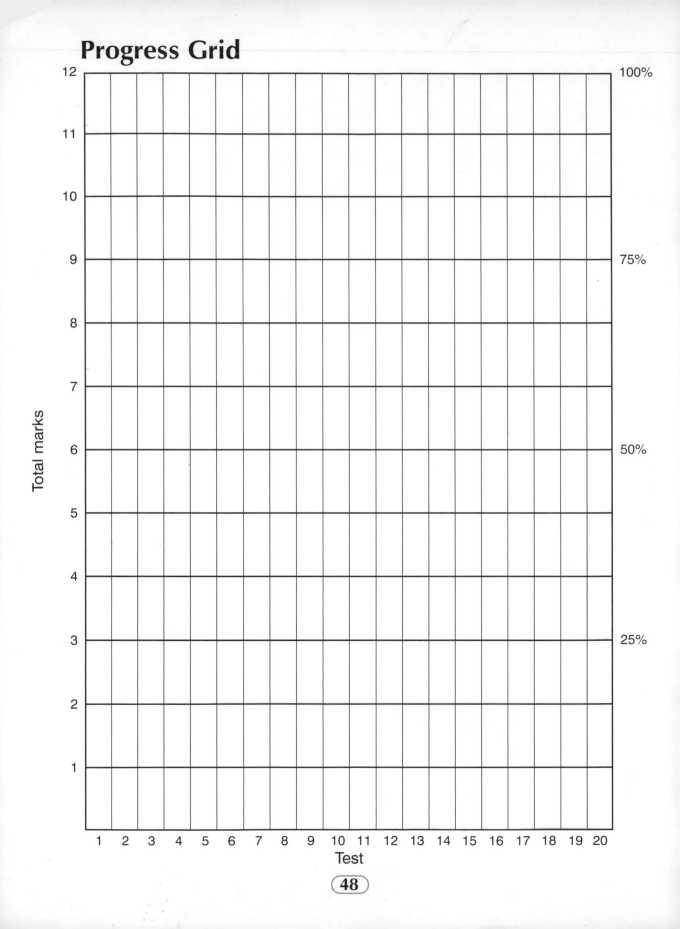

Total marks

Test